CAN I REALLY CHANGE THE WORLD?

One Voice Press
1233 Central Street, Evanston, IL 60201

Written and developed by Saman Maydani and Carlos Esparza in collaboration with Bahá'í Publishing.
 Published 2025
Printed in the United States of America ∞

28 27 26 25 1 2 3 4

Book and cover design by Carlos Esparza

ISBN 978-1-61851-266-6

. . . let your heart burn with loving kindness for all who may cross your path.

—*'Abdu'l-Bahá*

CONTENTS

What is this book?

This book is intended as an introduction to the Bahá'í Faith and its role in advancing society. Every reader is different, and we want to acknowledge that. Some will want the history and Bahá'í teachings first; some may want to skip straight to questions of society, environment, or politics. We encourage you to read in any order you like. We also want to encourage your exploration of the teachings in the context of your own life and activities. What would your life look like if you applied these teachings to it? What would your neighborhood look like if these ideas and principles were reflected there? Whether or not we call ourselves Bahá'ís, these teachings belong to all of us.

LET'S TALK ABOUT THE BASICS

What is the Bahá'í Faith?

It is not for him to pride himself who loveth his own country, but rather for him who loveth the whole world. The earth is but one country, and mankind its citizens.

—Bahá'u'lláh•

The Bahá'í Faith is the most recent world religion and began in 1844 in what was known as Persia (present-day Iran). It was founded by Bahá'u'lláh, Who came with a powerful and controversial message that at the time most people could not accept—we are all one. His teachings and laws were revealed to address our modern problems and bring about the peace and unity of the human race. Now, still less than 200 years since Bahá'u'lláh revealed His mission, our world is far more connected than anyone could have imagined back then. And even though it may still sometimes seem as though peace and progress are impossible, we have come a very long way in the short time since the Bahá'í Faith was founded. But there's still work to do!

In all avenues of life, the Bahá'í teachings address specifically how to bring about unity and prosperity for all. This book will give you an overview of those teachings in the context of our lives today and share how people worldwide are putting them into practice in their own communities.

What is a Bahá'í? Someone who believes in Bahá'u'lláh and His message and strives to put these principles into practice.

What does unity mean?

Another word for unity is *oneness*, but oneness does not mean sameness. Bahá'ís believe in the unity of humankind, of religion, and of God— a unity that celebrates our individuality and diversity. Bahá'ís believe that in the future we will live in unity and all strive together for the betterment of the world and all of humanity.

Bahá'u'lláh gave us teachings to bring unity into reality. They show us that by seeing humanity as one human family, we can eliminate prejudice of all kinds and bring about justice and freedom from opression for all peoples. The goal for all Bahá'ís is to align mankind in this vision, and to bring about an entirely new world civilization of peaceful coexistence for all living things. We believe that the enormous recent advancements in our society (communication, travel, scientific discovery) are all part of God's plan to unite humanity and create this new world.

Regard the world as the human body which, though at its creation whole and perfect, hath been afflicted, through various causes, with grave disorders and maladies.... That which the Lord hath ordained as the sovereign remedy and mightiest instrument for the healing of all the world is the union of all its peoples in one universal Cause, one common Faith. This can in no wise be achieved except through the power of a skilled, an all-powerful and inspired Physician.

—Bahá'u'lláh•

Who started the Bahá'í Faith? Is anyone in charge of it?

The Báb was the Forerunner of Bahá'u'lláh. He was born in 1819 as Siyyid 'Alí-Muhammad in Shiraz, Persia. Fulfilling Islamic prophecy, the Báb (Arabic title meaning "the Gate") prepared people for the coming of Bahá'u'lláh by bringing a unique set of teachings that broke from Islam. The Báb's message of oneness and spiritual independence was a threat to the clergy of the time. He and many of His followers were executed by those in power. Those who were not executed later became followers of Bahá'u'lláh.

Bahá'u'lláh was the Prophet and Founder of the Bahá'í Faith. The title *Bahá'u'lláh* means "the Glory of God" in Arabic. He was born Mírzá Ḥusayn-'Alí in 1817 in Tehran to a noble family. In His early years He became known for His innate wisdom and kindness. Eventually, He attracted so many followers that the clergy and royalty became threatened and exiled Him and His family out of the Persian Empire. Those in power, who had attempted in vain to snuff out the influence and message of the Báb, once again tried to do the same to Bahá'u'lláh. Yet, despite forty years of imprisonment, persecution, and exile, Bahá'u'lláh's message of peace has spread to every locality on the planet. He revealed the equivalent of over 100 volumes, and the writings and literature of His Faith have been translated into more than 800 languages. He passed away in 1892.

'Abdu'l-Bahá was the eldest son of Bahá'u'lláh. Born in 1844 and named Abbas Effendi, His father designated Him as His successor, and He served as the head of the Bahá'í

Faith from 1892 to 1921. The title *'Abdu'l-Bahá* means "Servant of the Glory," referencing His father. 'Abdu'l-Bahá was not a Prophet of God, but is often called "the Perfect Exemplar," meaning an example of human behavior that we can strive to follow. The essential sacred texts of the Bahá'í Faith are made up of prayers and other writings revealed by Bahá'u'lláh, the Báb, and 'Abdu'l-Bahá. 'Abdu'l-Bahá was also the chosen interpreter of His father's writings and spent much of His time teaching the Bahá'í Faith through speeches, travels, and correspondence.

Shoghi Effendi was the eldest grandson of 'Abdu'l-Bahá. In his grandfather's will, he was named the Guardian of the Bahá'í Faith—a role that he carried out from 1921 until his own passing in 1957. Like 'Abdu'l-Bahá, he was given the authority to interpret the Faith's sacred texts. In his role as the Guardian, he directed the affairs of the global Bahá'í community and oversaw the worldwide spread and growth of the Faith and its institutions. He paved the way for the election of the Universal House of Justice.

The Universal House of Justice is the international governing body of the Bahá'í Faith. It was described in the writings of Bahá'u'lláh, and further explained by both 'Abdu'l-Bahá and Shoghi Effendi. It is a globally elected institution that guides the direction and growth of the international Bahá'í community and rules on any matters that are not set forth explicitly in the sacred texts. It was established in 1963 and is voted for by representatives of the global Bahá'í community by silent ballot, without any campaigning or nominations, once every five years.

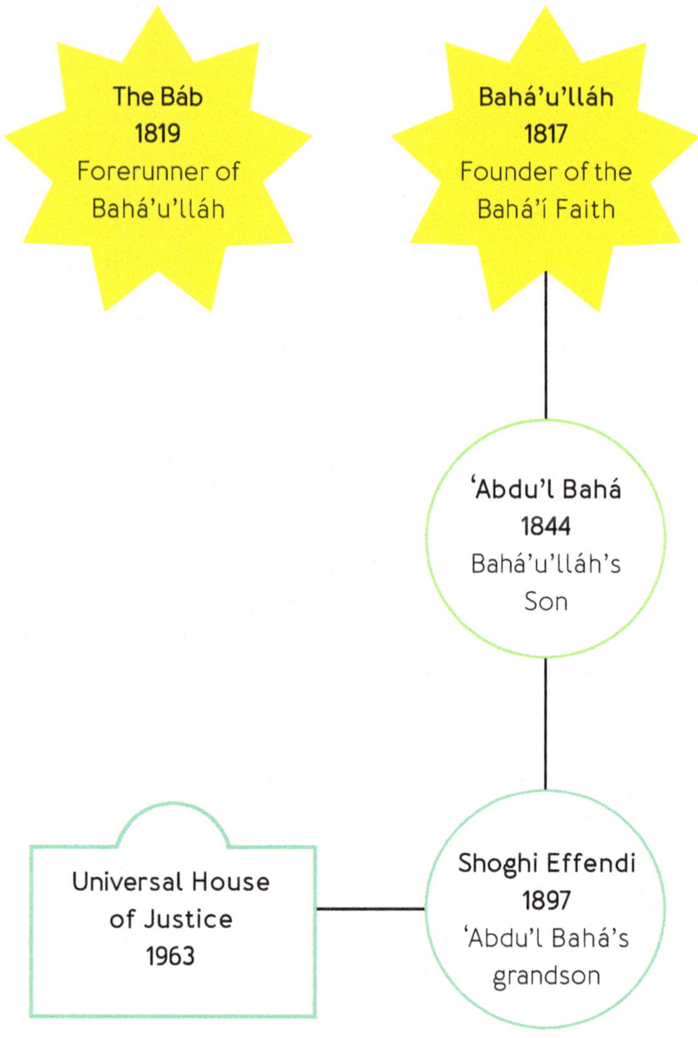
The Báb
1819
Forerunner of
Bahá'u'lláh
Bahá'u'lláh
1817
Founder of the
Bahá'í Faith
'Abdu'l Bahá
1844
Bahá'u'lláh's
Son
Shoghi Effendi
1897
'Abdu'l Bahá's
grandson
Universal House
of Justice
1963

Is the Bahá'í Faith a sect of another religion?

No, the Bahá'í Faith is an independent religion. It was founded in what is today Iran and emerged in a Muslim society in the same way that Christianity emerged in a Jewish one. Each of the world's major religions are independent from one another, but they are linked. From a Bahá'í perspective, all these religions are one:

> *We must recognize the sun, no matter from what dawning point it may shine forth, . . . for we are lovers of sunlight and not of orientation. We are lovers of illumination and not of lamps and candles.*

—*'Abdu'l-Bahá*•

According to the Bahá'í writings, each of the world's major religions can be seen as chapters in the same unfolding book. Essentially, there is only one religion, there is only one God, and each Prophet of the various religions was sent to reveal teachings and laws appropriate for the place and/or time in which They appeared. Bahá'u'lláh is the first Messenger sent to unite all of humanity.

Are there sects of the Bahá'í Faith?

No, there are no sects or separate branches permitted in the Bahá'í Faith. Bahá'u'lláh ensured there would be no sects by appointing as His successor His son, 'Abdu'l-Bahá, Who then named as His successors the Guardian and eventually the Universal House of Justice. For the Bahá'í Faith to be split into sects would be the antithesis of its core teaching of unity.

This unity is ensured by something known as the *Covenant*, which is another word for *agreement*. According to the Covenant of Bahá'u'lláh, the Bahá'í community will never be without guidance and leadership. There has been a clear line of succession from Bahá'u'lláh to 'Abdu'l-Bahá to Shoghi Effendi to the Universal House of Justice. And, for the Covenant to be effective, the members of the community must do their part and recognize the authority and leadership of the head of the Faith, which is now the Universal House of Justice. This not only ensures the unity of the Bahá'ís, it also means that the entire global community shares a common vision and works toward it in a coordinated manner.

This is one of the things that sets the Bahá'í Faith apart from religions of the past. Historically, when the Founders of the world's religions have died, Their religions quickly fractured into different sects as different people vied for power and had opposing views about what should happen next. The Covenant of Bahá'u'lláh is designed to avoid this problem.

Who or What is God?

That which we imagine is not the Reality of God; He, the Unknowable, the Unthinkable, is far beyond the highest conception of man.

—'Abdu'l-Bahá•

The Bahá'í teachings say that there is one God and that God is an unknowable essence. God has no gender, no race, no form—in fact, there is nothing in our human conception that can be applied to the Creator's reality. We may use language to describe "Him," because that's what humans do, so God has many names, but none of them define Him. All of this does not mean we can't experience a genuine personal connection with the Creator, or that we can know nothing about Him. In fact, quite the opposite—the Bahá'í teachings state that we were created to know and worship God.

So, how can we know an unknowable essence? Read on!

Can we know God?

The object of God's teaching to man is that man may know himself in order to comprehend the greatness of God.

—'Abdu'l-Bahá•

The Bahá'í Faith tells us that God communicates His purpose for humanity through Messengers or Manifestations, Whose qualities, examples, stories, and teachings give us access to what it means to know God, which in turn means to truly know ourselves and each other.

Baha'u'llah, the Manifestation of God for this day, says that God can be known through His attributes. These attributes are what we sometimes call virtues—things such as love, justice, kindness, generosity, and truthfulness. Bahá'u'lláh tells us that while all of creation can reflect certain attributes of God, humans are the only creatures that have the capacity to reflect all of them. But it is up to us whether or not we live up to this potential (that's called free will!). So, one way we can "know" God is by reflecting His attributes in our actions.

An analogy to help understand this concept is that of the light of the sun on a mirror. God is the sun and we are mirrors. If we face the sun, we can reflect the sun's light.

What is our place in relation to God?

> *The higher plane, however, understandeth the lower. The animal, for instance, comprehendeth the mineral and vegetable, the human understandeth the planes of the animal, vegetable and mineral. But the mineral cannot possibly understand the realms of man . . . no lower degree can ever comprehend a higher.*

—'Abdu'l-Bahá•

According to the Bahá'í teachings, just as humans are above the animal and the mineral (see the illustration on the next page), God and the Manifestations of God are above us. They understand us, and although our understanding of Them is limited, we can study writings and prayers to deepen it.

Remember, Manifestations are Messengers from God, sent to teach God's truth to humanity. Sometimes called Prophets, They bring the Word of God for Their age to humanity, and They are how we can begin to understand God. In the Bahá'í Faith the "Twin Manifestations" are the Báb and Bahá'u'lláh. They weren't God Himself, and They weren't ordinary men, but held a station in between.

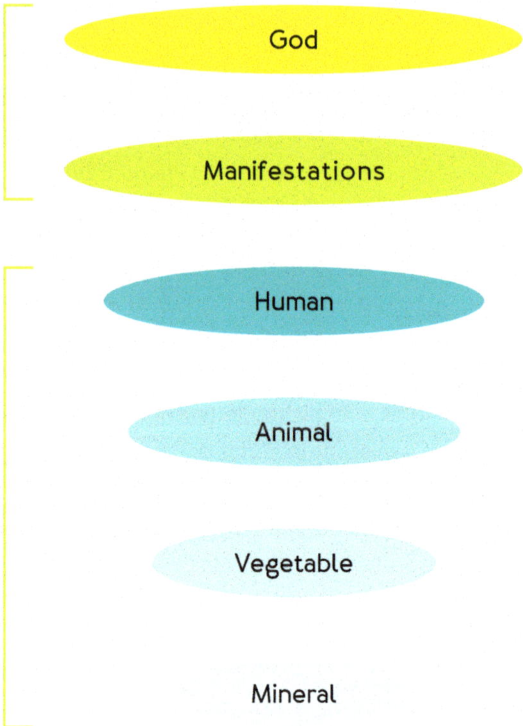
God
Manifestations
Human
Animal
Vegetable
Mineral

Do Bahá'ís have priests?

One very important principle of the Bahá'í Faith is the independent investigation of truth. This applies to every aspect of life—that we should always investigate things for ourselves and make up our own minds.

For this reason, Bahá'u'lláh abolished clergy of any kind. He teaches that we should each have our own direct relationship with God and that we can investigate truth for ourselves by reading the words of the Prophets or Manifestations..

> *[E]very individual member of humankind is exhorted and commanded to set aside superstitious beliefs, traditions and blind imitation of ancestral forms in religion and investigate reality for himself. Inasmuch as the fundamental reality is one, all religions and nations of the world will become one through investigation of reality.*

—'Abdu'l-Bahá•

Are there Bahá'í monks?

There are no monks in the Bahá'í Faith. In fact, monks are asked to leave the path of seclusion and quiet isolation and pursue a life of service to their communities and selves while enjoying and contributing to the benefits and beauty of this world.

> *O concourse of monks! Seclude not yourselves in your churches and cloisters. Come ye out of them by My leave, and busy, then, yourselves with what will profit you and others. Thus commandeth you He Who is the Lord of the Day of Reckoning.*

—Bahá'u'lláh[•]

What profits us and others? Luckily Bahá'u'lláh explains further:

> *It is enjoined upon every one of you to engage in some form of occupation, such as crafts, trades and the like. We have graciously exalted your engagement in such work to the rank of worship unto God, the True One.*

—Bahá'u'lláh[••]

What is prayer?

Bahá'ís believe that when we pray we are conversing with God. The act of prayer allows our souls to access the limitless power, love, and guidance of our Creator.

> *Prayer is the essential spiritual conversation of the soul with its Maker, direct and without intermediation. It is the spiritual food that sustains the life of the spirit. Like the morning's dew, it brings freshness to the heart and cleanses it, purifying it from attachments of the insistent self. It is a fire that burns away the veils and a light that leads to the ocean of reunion with the Almighty. On its wings does the soul soar in the heavens of God and draw closer to the divine reality.*
>
> —*The Universal House of Justice*•

In prayer we are often asking for clarity or for help. If our prayers take the form of questions, then in meditation we listen for the answers to apply to our individual lives and the life of our community.

> *The spirit of man is itself informed and strengthened during meditation; through it affairs of which man knew nothing are unfolded before his view. Through it he receives Divine inspiration.*
>
> —*'Abdu'l-Bahá*••

How do Bahá'ís pray?

Bahá'u'lláh, the Báb, and 'Abdu'l-Bahá all revealed prayers for many different occasions and needs, such as hardship, healing, protection, patience, children, gratitude, and commemorating the departed.

Bahá'ís can pray alone or in groups, silently or aloud, with eyes closed or open, spoken or in song, in words or even in action! All around the world Bahá'ís pray in whatever manner feels reverent to them—free from ritual. This is a necessary reflection of our global diversity! And the length of time you pray doesn't matter either—it's about sincerity.

> *Pride not yourselves on much reading of the verses or on a multitude of pious acts by night and day; for were a man to read a single verse with joy and radiance it would be better for him than to read with lassitude all the Holy Books of God.*
>
> —*Bahá'u'lláh*•

If a written prayer is being used, it is important that the meaning of the words be contemplated by the reader to discover the meaning for themselves in their life through the process of praying and meditating [see page 76]. For this reason, Bahá'í prayers have been translated into more than 800 different languages so that as many people as possible have access to these powerful words.

In short, Bahá'ís can pray any way they choose.

What's so special about religious texts?

Every word that proceedeth out of the mouth of God is endowed with such potency as can instill new life into every human frame.

*—Bahá'u'lláh**

Bahá'ís believe that the Word of God has creative power, a mysterious and mystical power that can inspire creativity and transformation within us. As Bahá'u'lláh tells us, the Word of God is "far higher and superior to that which the senses can perceive."**

Unlike many of the world's religions, the original written texts of the Báb, Bahá'u'lláh, and 'Abdu'l-Bahá still exist, and the translation of the texts from the original Persian and Arabic began during the lifetimes of the latter two. This means we have nearly direct access to these powerful words in their most accurate forms.

Another way to look at the importance of religious texts is to consider them "maps" for how we ought to act in our lives. Just as we must learn to read and interpret maps of geography, we must learn to read and apply the Word of God.

SOCIETY

Is the world falling apart?

Yes and no. The world is both falling apart and simultaneously being rebuilt. Bahá'ís believe that the great upheavals we see today are like the labor pains of a new world being born. Bahá'u'lláh warned us that the institutions that were built unjustly would one day crumble, and that in their place new and just ones must emerge. And Bahá'ís believe that our unity is not only possible but inevitable.

So, although distress and upheaval can be observed in many facets of society, all over the world people are learning how to build loving and just communities. This book is offered as a window and invitation to join the work of one such community. Bahá'ís all over the world are actively, joyfully working toward an inevitable outcome: peace and prosperity for all humankind.

We must expect these things: It is becoming evident that the world is not yet through with its labor, the New Age not yet fully born, real Peace not yet right around the corner. We must have no illusions about how much depends on us and our success or failure. All humanity is disturbed and suffering and confused; we cannot expect to not be disturbed and not to suffer—but we don't have to be confused. On the contrary, confidence and assurance, hope and optimism are our prerogative.

— From a letter written on behalf of Shoghi Effendi[•]

Is world peace possible? Can we save humanity?

Absolutely. The Bahá'í Faith may be dismissed by some as a utopian vision, but that's not accurate. Bahá'u'lláh is not simply calling for brotherly love alone, but a complete change in the structure of present-day society, a change "such as the world has not yet experienced."

> *It calls for no less than the reconstruction and the demilitarization of the whole civilized world . . .*
>
> *—Shoghi Effendi**

In Bahá'u'lláh's vision for society, He describes the structures and qualities for the future world. He tells Bahá'ís to "adhere tenaciously unto that which will promote fellowship, kindliness and unity."** There will be a global system of governance, unity among countries, a universal language (not to replace local languages, but an additional one to facilitate worldwide communication and connection), and universal education.

In other words, we can't imagine world peace because we are trying to imagine it in our world. The two don't work together! We must imagine a new kind of world, where peace is possible, and work toward that new world. And the good news is, we are not alone in this. In fact, the Universal House of Justice regularly provides detailed plans to help the Bahá'í global community translate these ideas into action.

What is the oneness of humanity?

In the Bahá'í Faith, all of humanity is seen as one human family.

> *This is one globe, one land, one country. God did not divide it into national boundaries. He created all the continents without national divisions.*
>
> —*'Abdu'l-Bahá**

Oneness does not mean that we are all the same. The Bahá'í vision of oneness is about embracing both our diversity and our interdependence.

Bahá'u'lláh uses another metaphor to describe the ultimate potential for our relation to one another—that of the human body. Our design is to work together as the cells of the human body, and only if we do can the body (humanity as a whole) ever hope to be truly healthy or happy.

> *Human society is composed not of a mass of merely differentiated cells but of associations of individuals, each one of whom is endowed with intelligence and will; . . . No cell lives apart from the body, whether in contributing to its functioning or in deriving its share from the well-being of the whole.*
>
> —*Bahá'í International Community***

If all religions are one, then why do they seem so different?

The Bahá'í Faith teaches a concept that may be new for many people: that there is only one religion, the religion of God. All major faiths are different chapters of that faith. Each religious Prophet or Manifestation throughout history—whether you take the example of Buddha, Moses, Jesus Christ, Muhammad, or Bahá'u'lláh—came to bring the same spiritual or moral messages. These messages are those we can see in one form or another in every religion on earth: "Regard your neighbor's gain as your own gain, and your neighbor's loss as your own loss," "Thou shall not kill," "Do not consume one another's property by unjust means."•

The differences emerge in the social teachings. They bring different laws and principles appropriate for new stages in humankind's development. Just as a parent may give different guidance to a child at different stages of their development, so too has God given humanity new laws at different times in history. In this way religion acts as a kind of school for humanity, evolving and growing with humanity to aid in our development along the arc of history. Another reason the world's religions look so different is that over time, spiritual lessons may be rewritten or misunderstood or manipulated by people, causing disunity, division, and prejudice between religions and sects. But Bahá'u'lláh had a plan to keep this from ever happening again. For more info on that, see page 10.

The Revelation of God may be likened to the sun. No matter how innumerable its risings, there is but one sun, and upon it depends the life of all things.

—the Báb[••]

If all the religions are one, then how many gods are there?

In the Bahá'í view, there is, and can only ever be one God. Even in the case of Hinduism, where it seems as though there are multiple gods, the various "gods" of that religion can be seen as symbolic manifestations of the divine attributes of the one God.

> *The Creator of all is One God.*
> *From this same God all creation sprang into existence, and He is the one goal, towards which everything in nature yearns.*
>
> —*'Abdu'l-Bahá*•

Why do people of different religions not get along?

The divine Prophets are conjoined in the perfect state of love. Each One has given the glad tidings of His successor's coming and each successor has sanctioned the One Who preceded Him. They were in the utmost unity, but Their followers are in strife. For instance, Moses gave the message of the glad tidings of Christ, and Christ confirmed the Prophethood of Moses. Therefore, between Moses and Jesus there is no variation or conflict.

—*'Abdu'l-Bahá**

At its root, the reason people of all religions don't get along often has more to do with political, social, and other issues than with the religions themselves. In our own limited way as individuals, we know how difficult it can be to let go of something we believe in, or to accept new information when it challenges what we believe.

'Abdu'l-Bahá reminds us that "Attachment to the lantern is not loving the light."** So we can see the message of God as the light, and each religion or religious text as the lanterns, and focus on our similarities, rather than our differences.

Why do we need a new religion?

This is a unique time in history. Turmoil surrounds so many issues—justice, politics, gender, race, economics, the environment, etc.—all of which are topics about which there is little very specific applicable guidance from previous religions. We are in need of renewal. The Bahá'í Faith is the most up-to-date "operating system" for the world.

> *Humanity is now experiencing the commotions invariably associated with the most turbulent stage of its evolution, the stage of adolescence, when the impetuosity of youth and its vehemence reach their climax, and must gradually be superseded by the calmness, the wisdom, and the maturity that characterize the stage of manhood.*

—*Shoghi Effendi*•

Humanity has come a long way and we are finally at a time where we can read the Word of God for ourselves and develop direct authentic personal relationships with the Divine. For this reason, Bahá'u'lláh abolished the clergy.

We have arrived at a stage of global interdependence. Technology is connecting us and showing us this interdependence like never before. Since we are now moving past adolescence toward the maturity of humanity, new social and spiritual teachings are needed in order for us to prosper. In short, our spiritual advancement needs to keep pace with our material advancement, or our society will lose its way.

Are there Bahá'í politicians?

No. Bahá'ís are forbidden from engaging in partisan politics. The current global political model is rooted in contention, picking sides, clinging to ideas, and vying for power. Because the whole system is at odds with Bahá'í principles of consultation, unity, and cooperation, Bahá'ís don't participate. While they can vote in political elections and support social causes, they do so without joining political parties or getting involved in political debates.

> *[Bahá'ís] can neither change nor help the world in any other way at present. . . . [I]f they build up the Bahá'í pattern they can offer it as a remedy when all else has failed. . . . We must build up our Bahá'í system, and leave the faulty systems of the world to go their way. We cannot change them through becoming involved in them; on the contrary, they will destroy us.*

—Shoghi Effendi•

There are Bahá'ís working in all spheres and professions, trying to bring the teachings into practice. The Bahá'í community is represented at all levels of society, including the United Nations, where members bring a Bahá'í perspective to discussions and actions focused on topics such as gender equality, social development, human rights, the environment, and peace and security.

What about war?

Basically, it's no good:

Wars—religious, racial or political—have arisen from human ignorance, misunderstanding and lack of education.

*—'Abdu'l-Bahá**

Every limited area which we call our native country we regard as our mother-land, whereas the terrestrial globe is the mother-land of all, and not any restricted area. In short, for a few days we live on this earth and eventually we are buried in it, it is our eternal tomb. Is it worthwhile that we should engage in bloodshed and tear one another to pieces for this eternal tomb? Nay, far from it, neither is God pleased with such conduct nor would any sane man approve of it.

*—'Abdu'l-Bahá***

A man who kills another man is punished by execution, but a military genius who kills one hundred thousand of his fellow creatures is immortalized as a hero. . . . Consider the ignorance and inconsistency of mankind.

*—'Abdu'l-Bahá****

What is justice?

Justice is the ability we each have to see beyond our own desires, to consider the needs of others, and treat one another fairly. This saves us from the traps of prejudice of all kinds, and hopefully from simply doing as others have done—instead thinking for ourselves and acting based on the promptings of our soul.

> *The purpose of justice is the appearance of unity among men.*
>
> —*Bahá'u'lláh*•

> *Just as forgiveness is one of the attributes of God's mercy, so is justice one of the attributes of His lordship. The canopy of existence rests upon the pole of justice and not of forgiveness, and the life of mankind depends on justice and not on forgiveness.*
>
> —*'Abdu'l-Bahá*••

Is equality possible when everybody is so different?

Equality does not mean sameness. The Bahá'í vision for unity is based on diversity.

The diversity in the human family should be the cause of love and harmony, as it is in music where many different notes blend together in the making of a perfect chord.

—*'Abdu'l-Bahá*•

Just like every cell in our body has a specialized function and unique location, every person in the human family is unique. Although people may each prefer very different environments or lifestyles, they each have universal human rights and should expect their basic human needs to be met.

Love all from the depths of your hearts, prefer all religionists before yourselves, be filled with love for every race, and be kind toward the people of all nationalities. Never speak disparagingly of others, but praise without distinction.

—*'Abdu'l-Bahá*••

Equality is possible if we each foster love in our hearts even for those most different from us.

What is prejudice?

'Abdu'l-Bahá tells us that prejudice is blind imitation of the past—which makes sense. When we "pre-judge" somebody or something, we're not taking the time to learn for our own selves and discover the truth as it applies to us or to our individual experience. When this happens on a community or societal level, BIG problems can occur.

> *It is evident that prejudices arising from adherence to religious forms and imitation of ancestral beliefs have hindered the progress of humanity thousands of years. How many wars and battles have been fought, how much division, discord and hatred have been caused by this form of prejudice!*
>
> —*'Abdu'l-Bahá**

> *So free must be your thoughts and actions of any trace of prejudice—racial, religious, economic, national, tribal, class, or cultural—that even the stranger sees in you loving friends.*
>
> —*The Universal House of Justice***

What does the Bahá'í Faith say about racism?

In the Bahá'í writings, racism is described as "the most vital and challenging issue"* in American society.

Both Shoghi Effendi and 'Abdu'l-Bahá wrote at length about the challenge of racism in America and unifying Black and white. 'Abdu'l-Bahá stated that if the situation were not remedied, "the streets of American cities [would] run with blood,"** and, urging unity, is reported to have said that it could lead to the destruction of America.***

Writing about the problem of anti-Black racism, Shoghi Effendi called for great effort on the part of both white and Black people:

> *Let neither think that the solution of so vast a problem is a matter that exclusively concerns the other. Let neither think that such a problem can either easily or immediately be resolved. Let neither think that they can wait confidently for the solution of this problem until the initiative has been taken, and the favorable circumstances created, by agencies that stand outside the orbit of their Faith. Let neither think that anything short of genuine love, extreme patience, true humility, consummate tact, sound initiative, mature wisdom, and deliberate, persistent, and prayerful effort, can succeed in blotting out the stain which this patent evil has left on the fair name of their common country.*

*—Shoghi Effendi*****

Racism, one of the most baneful and persistent evils, is a major barrier to peace. Its practice perpetrates too outrageous a violation of the dignity of human beings to be countenanced under any pretext. Racism retards the unfoldment of the boundless potentialities of its victims, corrupts its perpetrators, and blights human progress. Recognition of the oneness of mankind, implemented by appropriate legal measures, must be universally upheld if this problem is to be overcome.

—The Universal House of Justice[•••••]

Do Bahá'ís care about the equality of the sexes?

Bahá'u'lláh is the only Manifestation of God to unequivocally state that men and women are equal and that the advancement of women is essential. He made provisions in His laws to promote this reality.

> *Until the reality of equality between man and woman is fully established and attained, the highest social development of mankind is not possible. . . .*
>
> —*'Abdu'l-Bahá*[*]

> *As long as women are prevented from attaining their highest possibilities, so long will men be unable to achieve the greatness which might be theirs.*
>
> —*'Abdu'l-Bahá*[**]

'Abdu'l-Bahá teaches that the future will be an age in which the "masculine and feminine elements of civilization will be more evenly balanced." Specifically He says that the qualities in which women are stronger than men, mental alertness, intuition, and the spiritual qualities of love and service will permeate the coming age, and shift the scales away from masculine dominance.[***]

The world of humanity is possessed of two wings—the male and the female. So long as these two wings are not equivalent in strength the bird will not fly. Until womankind reaches the same degree as man, until she enjoys the same arena of activity, extraordinary attainment for humanity will not be realized; humanity cannot wing its way to heights of real attainment

—*'Abdu'l-Bahá*••••

As with everything Bahá'u'lláh foresaw and taught, we are now seeing this rebalancing between the feminine and masculine elements playing out in all arenas of life.

Woman must be given the privilege of equal education with man and full right to his prerogatives.... In truth, she will be the greatest factor in establishing universal peace and international arbitration. Assuredly, woman will abolish warfare among mankind.

—*'Abdu'l-Bahá*•••••

One example of Bahá'u'lláh's laws on this topic is that, if a Bahá'í parent has to make the difficult choice of educating a daughter or a son (for financial reasons perhaps), the daughter must receive preference—breaking from all traditions of the past.

COMMUNITY

What is Bahá'í life/culture like?

The simple answer is that there is no singular "Bahá'í culture." Bahá'í life is as varied and diverse as the many cultures represented in the global community. Bahá'u'lláh did away with all rituals and traditions of previous religions, which allows for people to bring their authentic selves into the practice of their faith. He did, however, reveal certain laws and practices that create a framework for Bahá'í community life.

> *And the honor and distinction of the individual consist in this, that he among all the world's multitudes should become a source of social good.*
>
> *—'Abdu'l-Bahá*

Bahá'ís all over the world are engaged in building community. From a Bahá'í perspective, all the principles and teachings of the Faith are only truly meaningful when translated into action. Bahá'ís invite their friends and neighbors to join them in applying the Faith's teachings to their individual lives as well as to the collective life of their neighborhood or community.

What does this look like? Currently, in neighborhoods all over the world, you will find Bahá'ís and their friends taking part in study circles (p. 49), devotional gatherings (p. 50), children's classes (p. 45), junior youth groups (p. 46), and service projects. Music and the arts are often a big part of these activities.

Why have a religious community?

The Bahá'í community is distinguished by a shared sense of purpose. Other, non-religious types of communities (schools, workplaces, neighborhoods, or even cities) might sometimes band together to work toward a common goal or vision, but it is not the norm. If partisan politics is not the answer (see page 30), then activities at the community level are the best way to make a change in the world.

> *Because religion has historically shown an unrivaled capacity both to unite disparate peoples in a shared sense of identity and purpose and also to divide them against one another with disastrous consequences, the role of faith communities in society is critical.*
>
> *—Office of Public Affairs, US Bahá'í National Organization*•

Bahá'ís believe that community is the training ground for discovering how to live the principles of the Faith as a society; what humanity collectively learns at the community level helps to show us the road to peace.

Naturally, so much about the Bahá'í Faith, as with any other religion, begins with the individual practice of the Faith. We'll get to that on page 53. For now, let us consider how individuals engage in the Faith at the community level.

So much of what Bahá'ís do is at the community level as individuals striving to put the Bahá'í teachings into practice collectively.

What kinds of things do Bahá'í communities do?

The focus in Bahá'í communities, encouraged and guided by the Universal House of Justice, is to engage in what is known as the "core activities." These are children's classes, junior youth groups, study circles, and devotional gatherings. We'll learn more about each of those in a moment. First, let's talk about why these are the core activities.

The Bahá'í vision, as we mentioned earlier, is to create a new, peaceful world—one that benefits each member of society. Rather than focusing on reaching that end through purely material means, Bahá'ís focus on building strong relationships with people who wish to work together to build a united world based on an understanding of our spiritual reality.

At the heart of this vision is interaction with the what Bahá'ís refer to as the Creative Word of God—the sacred Writings of the Manifestations. All of the core activities mentioned above involve engagement with the Creative Word, through prayer and devotions, study and reflection, and the application of insights to service and ongoing learning within the community.

By working and learning to better ourselves, while also helping those in our community to learn and grow along with us, we all have the power to change humanity.

You may notice that two of these core activities directly involve young people. Bahá'ís believe that youth are in a unique position to make the world a better, more just place, and have great potential to do so. See p. 47 for more about the role of youth.

What are children's classes?

Among the greatest of all services that can possibly be rendered by man to Almighty God is the education and training of children . . .

*—'Abdu'l-Bahá**

[I]t is in early childhood that a firm foundation must be laid. While the branch is green and tender it can easily be made straight. Our meaning is that qualities of the spirit are the basic and Divine foundation, and adorn the true essence of man; and knowledge is the cause of human progress. The beloved of God must attach great importance to this matter, and carry it forward with enthusiasm and zeal.

*—'Abdu'l-Bahá***

Children's classes are organized by Bahá'ís for kids roughly between the ages of five and eleven, regardless of whether they are members of the Bahá'í Faith. Activities include learning stories, singing songs, saying prayers, playing games, and arts and crafts. The only goal is pretty simple: to teach children about the power of ideas such as love, generosity, unity, and community, and to explore how to put these ideas into action in their lives.

What are junior youth groups?

Junior youth groups exist to channel the creativity and brilliance of people between the ages of twelve and fifteen into their communities to make constructive change.

Bahá'ís consider young people to be in a unique position to change the world, and, to make this possible, capacities must be identified and strengthened early on. In junior youth groups, friends begin to think about their purpose and the role they can play in serving and advancing humanity. They also learn to realize, appreciate, and advocate for their own worth. These groups study spiritual concepts and social issues together, engage in artistic projects, play cooperative games, and design and engage in acts of service. The facilitators of the groups are known as animators, and are often older youth.

Groups of friends coming together to build capacity to serve humanity and in time tackle the issues facing our planet and everybody on it!

While global trends project an image of this age group as problematic, lost in the throes of tumultuous physical and emotional change, unresponsive and self-consumed, the Bahá'í community—in the language it employs and the approaches it adopts—is moving decidedly in the opposite direction, seeing in junior youth instead altruism, an acute sense of justice, eagerness to learn about the universe and a desire to contribute to the construction of a better world.

*—The Universal House of Justice**

What about older teenagers and young adults?

So we've covered children's classes and junior youth groups, but that only brings us up to the age of fifteen, right? Does it all stop there? Far from it! Bahá'ís often refer to people roughly between the ages of fifteen and thirty as "youth," and the writings of the Faith have a lot to say about youth and their power to move the world!

> *When the exalted figure of the Báb, aged just twenty-five, arose to deliver His revolutionizing message to the world, many among those who accepted and spread His teachings were young, even younger than the Báb Himself. Their heroism . . . will illumine the annals of human history for centuries to come. Thus began a pattern in which every generation of youth, drawing inspiration from the same divine impulse to cast the world anew, has seized the opportunity to contribute to the latest stage in the unfolding process that is to transform the life of humankind. It is a pattern that has suffered no interruption from the time of the Báb to this present hour.*
>
> —*The Universal House of Justice*•

Youth have always been at the forefront of Bahá'í-inspired community-building efforts. Right now, youth all over the world are engaged in teaching children's classes, facilitating junior youth groups, participating in study circles, hosting devotional gatherings, and so many other initiatives focused on constructive social change. It is a unique time of life full of vitality and flexibility and when youth devote their time and energy to helping those younger than themselves develop the personal capacities and attitudes needed to advance society, the results are transformative for them, for the younger generations they are helping, and for the wider communities to which they belong.

What is a study circle?

Study circles refer to groups of people coming together to study materials that will enable them to walk a path of service together. Each of us walks this path at our own pace, but the members of a study circle support one another and share the journey. There are two general goals for the participants: to attend to their own individual spiritual and intellectual growth, and to contribute to the transformation of society.

There is a series of books being used in study circles all over the world. The topics cover a lot of the ground we're covering in this book, but in much greater depth. Topics include things like prayer, strengthening friendships and other relationships, the education of children, family dynamics, and acts of service for your community. The focus is always on studying the Creative Word of God, striving to understand it together, and gaining insights to be applied in acts of service.. For example, study circle participants learn to teach neighborhood children's classes, facilitate junior youth groups, and host devotional gatherings. The process is open to anyone interested in exploring concepts from the Bahá'í writings and putting them into practice in their lives and in the collective life of their community.

What about devotional gatherings?

An important facet of the Bahá'í Faith is the personal connection to God we can experience when we pray. We are encouraged to pray often on our own and to develop that personal connection throughout our daily life, but there is a special atmosphere created when we come together with others to pray and meditate in our neighborhood or community.

> *[W]here many are gathered together their force is greater. Separate soldiers fighting alone and individually have not the force of a united army.*
>
> *—Attributed to 'Abdu'l-Bahá*

A devotional gathering can involve a group of any size and often includes music and other artistic expressions in a reverent and prayerful atmosphere.

The idea is to deepen relationships and learn and be inspired by one another. Remember, in the Bahá'í Faith there is no prescribed way to pray, and there is a lot of room for creativity and expression. These events include people from other faith traditions and practices as well as those with no faith practices.

How does all this help with real problems that the world is facing?

Have you heard the phrase "think global, act local"? Well, all the activities above are meant to raise the capacity of communities so that they can address their own social, material, and spiritual issues. By building skills and community from a young age, the social action that results is embedded in the realities of a community and undertaken with an understanding of the world as one interconnected whole.

By coming together and learning how to transform themselves and their communities, people are able to apply their learning to all kinds of social issues.

Bahá'ís are involved in all types of social action, from climate change, to gender equality, to economic reform, to racial justice—and the list goes on.

What is service?

Service to humanity is service to God. Let the love and light of the Kingdom radiate through you until all who look upon you shall be illumined by its reflection. Be as stars, brilliant and sparkling in the loftiness of their heavenly station.

—*'Abdu'l-Bahá**

For Bahá'ís, service can take many forms. You may be involved, alongside members of your community, in service projects such as picking up garbage from your neighborhood, helping the poor, volunteering your time, and donating to a charity.

Anything you see in your world that could be improved in your view is a potential service project, but so is developing your own skills and building a profession. And all the core activities mentioned in the previous sections are all about service. When we are empowering ourselves and others to become active agents in the transformation of our lives and communities, we are being of service!

It is enjoined upon every one of you to engage in some form of occupation, such as crafts, trades and the like. We have graciously exalted your engagement in such work to the rank of worship unto God, the True One. . . . Waste not your time in idleness and sloth. Occupy yourselves with that which profiteth yourselves and others.

— *Bahá'u'lláh***

What about us as individuals?

All Bahá'í activity is centered around transforming both oneself and society at the same time, through work in the community. Neither can be accomplished without the other. So far, we've been discussing those larger ideas of society and community because they can have such a big impact on us as individuals, but we can also have a big impact on our communities and society through the activities we've just discussed!

> *We cannot segregate the human heart from the environment outside us and say that once one of these is reformed everything will be improved. Man is organic with the world. His inner life moulds the environment and is itself deeply affected by it. The one acts upon the other and every abiding change in the life of man is the result of these mutual reactions.*

—From a letter written on behalf of Shoghi Effendi•

While service to each other in community is a big part of Bahá'í life, a lot of our daily efforts must be focused on our own personal growth and development so we can be our best selves in those public spaces.

INDIVIDUAL

Who am I?

According to the Bahá'í writings you are a complex being with both a higher and a lower nature—spiritual and material, soul and body. You were created noble, and that nobility is what we aim to maintain in ourselves and to see and encourage in others. The key is to focus and have our higher nature calling the shots, so we may experience peace and spiritual prosperity.

> *[I]f . . . [man's] thought does not soar, but is directed downwards to center itself upon the things of this world, he grows more and more material until he arrives at a state little better than that of a mere animal.*
>
> —*'Abdu'l-Bahá*•

But it isn't always that easy to focus on spirituality or nobility, especially given how much of our lower or material nature is reflected back to us, and how little press our higher nature gets. Look around you. Society is focused mostly on our material aspects, the animal side of ourselves—your body shape, what you wear, where you live, what type of home you have, what you eat, your material wealth (or lack thereof). The list goes on and on.

But we are spiritual beings living in a material reality. Our job is to work within that rubric every day, to find unity with these different aspects of ourselves, and to not get lost.

What is the soul?

Bahá'ís believe that each of us has a soul, a nonphysical part of ourselves that is created in the image of the Creator with the capacity to reflect all His attributes. It has eternal life, it has no gender, and each one has been gifted with unique qualities and capacities to give the world. As opposed to the ego and its animal characteristics, the soul is noble.

The idea that we are created in the image of the Creator does not mean that the Creator has a physical body like we do, but that we have the capacity to reflect His divine attributes: honesty, justice, generosity, forgiveness, love, and wisdom, to name just a few examples.

> *The soul is not a combination of elements, it is not composed of many atoms, it is of one indivisible substance and therefore eternal. It is entirely out of the order of the physical creation; it is immortal!*
>
> —*'Abdu'l-Bahá*•

Bahá'ís believe that the soul comes into being with the conception of the body, and is connected with the body as light is with a mirror. If the mirror were broken, the light would remain. You cannot destroy a soul—it is eternal.

What is the purpose of life?

The Bahá'í perspective is that the soul is here to develop its attributes, by being of service to humanity, to help better this world, and in doing so prepare itself to take spiritual capacities into the next world, after death.

'Abdu'l-Bahá tells us that "that which he [humankind] needs in the world of the Kingdom must be obtained here,"• and likens this world to a womb in which we prepare for a birth into a more expansive reality.

> *Let each morn be better than its eve and each morrow richer than its yesterday. Man's merit lieth in service and virtue and not in the pageantry of wealth and riches.*
>
> —*Bahá'u'lláh*••

Developing our character is not something that we can do in isolation or by focusing on the self alone. The only way to truly grow and improve our character is in service to other people. That is where we are tested the most and can find where our work is.

How do we develop our attributes and virtues?

To start, by telling the truth.

> *Truthfulness is the foundation of all human virtues. Without truthfulness, progress and success, in all the worlds of God, are impossible for any soul. When this holy attribute is established in man, all the divine qualities will also be acquired.*
>
> —*'Abdu'l-Bahá*•

But there's more to it than telling the truth. We must value truthfulness in all its forms. This means seeking the truth through our own independent investigation of all things, and being honest with ourselves when considering what about ourselves can be improved!

Developing any virtue—whether it is truthfulness, trustworthiness, kindness, patience, loyalty—requires us to reflect on the meaning of the virtue and what it looks like in our lives, and to continue to try and put it into practice from day to day.

What's the deal with the body?

Even though our eternal self is spiritual, Bahá'ís do not believe in focusing solely on the nonphysical and in waiting for an afterlife while neglecting this one. Our material lives, including our bodies, are to be given the utmost respect and care so that we can carry out our individual design and be of service while we are here and benefit from and enjoy the wonders of this world.

The Baha'i teachings emphasize the importance of relying on medical professionals when we are ill [see p. 88], but also highlight the importance of diet and the healing properties of foods and herbs.•

> *Healing through purely spiritual forces is undoubtedly as inadequate as that which materialist physicians and thinkers vainly seek to obtain by resorting entirely to mechanical devices and methods. The best result can be obtained by combining the two processes: spiritual and physical.*
>
> *—From a letter written on behalf of Shoghi Effendi*••

This shows again the Bahá'í focus on both material and spiritual matters.

What is the ego?

In conventional psychological writing, the ego is the mediator between our instincts and our internal observer. In practical terms, the ego is concerned with the survival of the body. It fears death and requires separation from others to create a "sense of self." But the soul knows eternity. It does not fear death. It knows the reality of oneness with all.

The ego looks to satisfy our material desires and justify them to ourselves and/or those around us.

Anger, passion, ignorance, prejudice, greed, envy, covetousness, jealousy and suspicion prevent man from ascending to the realms of holiness, imprisoning him in the claws of self and the cage of egotism.

*— Attributed to 'Abdu'l-Bahá**

One of our primary jobs in life is to control our ego so that we are not ruled by it, and instead strive to live up to our higher nature. Meditation and prayer are among the means to control our ego.

Meditate profoundly, that the secret of things unseen may be revealed unto you, . . . so that light may be distinguished from darkness, truth from falsehood, right from wrong, guidance from error, happiness from misery, and roses from thorns.

*—Bahá'u'lláh***

What are mental health and mental illness?

Mental health can be thought of similarly to our physical health. We exercise our body so that we can be strong and in control of our bodies. We eat the right things for us to feel good and have lots of energy. Similarly, for mental health we can exercise our control of thoughts and focus on things that are going to help feed our higher nature.

Meditation and mindfulness are two of many tools available to us to help us stay grounded in the present while envisioning a positive future. Sometimes we need help to break patterns of thought and action so we can grow and develop, and sometimes we may need medical help. Bahá'ís may also seek out and receive support and care from professionals, such as psychiatrists and psychologists, as in all things Bahá'u'lláh advises us to consult medical experts.

> *It is very hard to be subject to any illness, particularly a mental one. However, we must always remember these illnesses have nothing to do with our spirit or our inner relation to God.*
>
> *—From a letter written on behalf of Shoghi Effendi*•

Is there life after death?

According to the Bahá'í Faith, yes!

> *The world beyond is as different from this world as this world is different from that of the child while still in the womb of its mother.*

*—Bahá'u'lláh**

From conception to birth we are protected inside our mother; we grow our eyes and limbs, hands and organs, everything we need for our time on earth. During our life on earth, we develop our spiritual capacities: truthfulness, humility, love, purity, trustworthiness, and so on—everything we need for our life in the next world, after death.

Just as we could never, in the womb, understand the material world, we cannot understand or envision the spiritual world we will enter after our physical body dies. Bahá'ís do not believe in the existence of a physical heaven or hell, and instead take these as symbolic terms to refer to nearness and distance from the Creator in this world and the realms beyond.

Bahá'í teachings specifically tell us that reincarnation, as it is often thought of, does not occur, but rather that our souls continue to progress in spiritual worlds beyond this one:

> *We come on to this planet once only.*

*—From a letter written on behalf of Shoghi Effendi***

Why do bad things happen?

Bahá'ís believe that difficulties can come to us in life for two reasons, either because of humanity's free will or as simple accidents. In either case, we can grow stronger as a result. For this reason, it is said that people should actually be "thankful in adversity"• to acknowledge that the experience will surely teach us something about ourselves or the world if we are open to learning the lesson.

> *The more difficulties one sees in the world the more perfect one becomes. The more you plough and dig the ground the more fertile it becomes. The more you cut the branches of a tree the higher and stronger it grows. The more you put the gold in the fire the purer it becomes . . . Therefore I am happy that you have had great tribulations and difficulties. . . . Strange it is that I love you and still I am happy that you have sorrows.*
>
> —*'Abdu'l-Bahá*••

Does evil exist?

Not exactly. Bahá'ís do not believe in the concept of evil, the devil, or evil supernatural figures.

> *Whatsoever God has created, He has created good. Evil consists merely in nonexistence . . . Good has a positive existence; evil is merely its absence.*

—'Abdu'l-Bahá•

One way to understand this "nonexistence" of evil is to compare it to darkness. Darkness does not exist as a physical entity; it is simply the absence of light.

In this same way, Bahá'ís do not believe that there is evil, nor a devil or Satan. These terms from previous revelations, Bahá'u'lláh has clarified, are simply symbols for the insistent self, the lower instincts of human nature, or the ego.

Even though our lower natures have considerable effect on the earth and each other, Bahá'ís are taught not to focus on other people's shortcomings, but rather to tame our own lower natures. Instead of pointing out the darkness, we should turn on the lights.

What is our intelligence for?

The sciences and arts, all inventions, crafts, trades and their products have come forth from the intellect of man. It is evident that within the human organism the intellect occupies the supreme station.

*—'Abdu'l-Bahá**

Bahá'ís are taught that "the reality of man is his thought, not his material body."** Our intelligence gives us the capacity to interpret the world around us, navigate it, and either have a positive impact or a negative one.

In the Bahá'í writings there are a number of deceptively simple teachings, such as: "A thought of hatred must be destroyed by a more powerful thought of love."*** The writings also call on us to make an effort "to suppress every critical thought and every harsh word."**** If we understand that "evil" is only an absence of peace and love, AND we understand that we have the power to create a better world, we must realize that the process begins with our thoughts. If we are careful about our thoughts, what we choose to think about, and what we choose to direct our creative energies toward, we can surely change the world around us.

What about sexuality?

> *We are not ascetics in any sense of the word. On the contrary, Bahá'u'lláh says God has created all the good things in the world for us to enjoy and partake. But we must not become attached to them and put them before the spiritual things.*

— From a letter written on behalf of Shoghi Effendi•

From a Bahá'í perspective, sexuality has been overemphasized to an unhealthy degree in modern society. Sexuality is a natural and healthy part of being human, but it should not dominate our lives and thoughts. The Bahá'í teachings state that sexuality should find a healthy expression within the context of marriage, and that Bahá'ís should remain chaste outside of marriage. While marriage is defined in the Bahá'í writings as between a man and woman, Bahá'ís do not judge or impose such expectations on others. Doing so would be contrary to the spirit and teachings of the Faith.

Similarly, judging or imposing expectations on somebody's sexual orientation or gender identity is contrary to the Faith's teachings. Each person's journey is their own responsibility.

What does the Bahá'í Faith say about gender identity?

Bahá'u'lláh is clear on the matter of our eternal souls having no gender. But as people in the world, we do have gender, and it is undoubtedly true that our reception by the world—whether for reasons of gender identity or any other—can deeply affect our daily experience of life. The imposed expectations on each of us concerning our identity can affect our mental health if we are not careful to work through any challenges that may arise.

The question is: how much do our experiences surrounding these issues affect our ability to pursue our spiritual path? Does our gender identity affect the purpose of life? Will our reception in the world as any given gender enhance or inhibit our ability to grow and increase our spiritual capacities?

While the Bahá'í writings ask us to dress and act in moderation, there are no specific guidelines regarding social gender expression. Bahá'ís are encouraged not to place undue focus on the aspects of identity that are impermanent; however, such matters are left to individual discretion, and the teachings of the Faith call for an attitude of acceptance, respect, and love for all.

Also, the Universal House of Justice tells us that "Bahá'í institutions would not specifically counsel believers on the advisability or inadvisability of undergoing a sex change,"• which is a medical issue. As with all Bahá'í teachings, love, acceptance, and compassion for all souls is paramount, and consultation with family members and loved ones is encouraged whenever possible.

Can we judge others?

Well, we are supposed to have concern for others, and do everything in our power to serve our fellow humans. But . . .

> *Whenever you recognize the fault of another, think of yourself! What are my imperfections? . . . Thus you will grow, become more perfect. . . . you will not even have time to think of the faults of others.*

—'Abdu'l-Bahá*

To put it simply: We must not worry about others' faults, or our thoughts about others (judgments or prejudices). In the Bahá'í Faith, talking about others is known as backbiting, or in other words: gossiping. This is a subject which is absolute in the Bahá'í writings; no ifs, ands, or buts about it: it is strictly forbidden.

> *Backbiting quencheth the light of the heart, and extinguisheth the life of the soul.*

—Bahá'u'lláh**

We all likely know from experience, that backbiting leads to hurt feelings, distrust, and disunity. When we are trying to build community and create unity, there is simply no room for it.

Can we compare ourselves to others?

Whether or not we have better developed skills or even an innate ability in one area or another, we cannot allow our God-given talents to change our view of ourselves compared to anybody else. We may be better at something than somebody else, but that does not make us better than somebody else.

> *He must never seek to exalt himself above any one, must wash away from the tablet of his heart every trace of pride and vain-glory.*
>
> —*Bahá'u'lláh*•

If our focus is on our own greatness and increasing it, we may or may not succeed temporarily, but we will be in constant turmoil—feeling either very great or not good enough. If, on the other hand, we focus on helping others and increasing their ability, we will all improve together as a community, and we will always feel better for having helped somebody.

So, we're just supposed to be nice and offer help to everyone?

It's a little more involved than that:

You must manifest complete love and affection toward all mankind. Do not exalt yourselves above others, but consider all as your equals, recognizing them as the servants of one God. Know that God is compassionate toward all; therefore, love all from the depths of your hearts, prefer all religionists before yourselves, be filled with love for every race, and be kind toward the people of all nationalities. Never speak disparagingly of others, but praise without distinction. Pollute not your tongues by speaking evil of another. Recognize your enemies as friends, and consider those who wish you evil as the wishers of good . . . Beware! Beware! lest ye offend any heart. Assist the world of humanity as much as possible. Be the source of consolation to every sad one, assist every weak one, be helpful to every indigent one, care for every sick one, be the cause of glorification to every lowly one, and shelter those who are overshadowed by fear.

In brief, let each one of you be as a lamp shining forth with the light of the virtues of the world of humanity. Be trustworthy, sincere, affectionate and replete with chastity. Be illumined, be spiritual, be divine, be glorious, be quickened of God, be a Bahá'í.

—*'Abdu'l-Bahá*•

MORE TEACHINGS

Does the Bahá'í Faith have any rules?

Yes! Just as with every faith and spiritual practice before it, the Bahá'í Faith also has laws. These laws address the spiritual and material needs of today, with the goal of creating unity between all of humanity and bringing peace, prosperity, and happiness to those who follow them.

His Law is a fortress unto you, could ye but understand.

*—Bahá'u'lláh**

Bahá'u'lláh came to set humanity free. His Revelation is, indeed, an invitation to freedom—freedom from want, freedom from war, freedom to unite, freedom to progress, freedom in peace and joy.

*—The Universal House of Justice***

Laws give us freedom? Yes!

One way to understand laws is to think about them as a boundary being given to us by a loving parent. Laws are seen as a protection for us personally but also as guideposts to help us achieve unity in the world. This is similar to the way that streetlights and stop signs give us structure, protection, and a shared understanding of how to drive safely. Those are the kinds of laws that few of us, if any, would question.

What are some Bahá'í laws?

Since the Bahá'í Faith is the most recent in a series of progressive revelations, many laws from the past still apply. We could probably refer to these as the obvious ones: no killing, no stealing . . . you get the idea.

There are some others that have been in previous religions too and some that are relatively new, or in a new form in the Bahá'í Faith: no sex outside of marriage, no gambling, no alcohol or drugs. Daily prayer is also prescribed as a requirement as well as reading and meditating on the Bahá'í writings. Bahá'ís also take part in a period of fasting once a year.

What about when a Bahá'í dies? Well, their body cannot be transported more than an hour's journey from where they died. The body cannot be cremated or embalmed; it must be washed and then wrapped in silk or cotton.

Another law is a STRICT prohibition on backbiting. (See page 69 for more on that!)

These are just a few examples of Bahá'í laws. All of them are contained in a book called the Kitáb-i-Aqdas, or the Most Holy Book, revealed by Bahá'u'lláh.

Do Bahá'ís have to pray?

When we turn to God with our whole heart and invoke His Name, a spiritual connection is established through which we become a channel of divine influence.

*—From a letter written on behalf of Shoghi Effendi**

The purpose of prayer is to connect with our Creator, to ask questions about life and receive inspiration to then apply to our personal lives and practice in community with others. It is the foundation of Bahá'í life. We are reminded to keep it authentic and personal when connecting with the Word and the Creator.

[W]ere a man to read a single verse with joy and radiance it would be better for him than to read with lassitude all the Holy Books of God . . .

*—Bahá'u'lláh***

In addition to the many prayers (see page 18, "How do Bahá'ís pray?") Bahá'u'lláh revealed for different occasions, He also revealed a special set of prayers called obligatory prayers. While use of other revealed prayers is left to the discretion of the individual in their daily devotions, the recitation of a daily obligatory prayer is a Bahá'í law.

There are three different obligatory prayers to choose from. They vary in length, but all three are equally acceptable.

Bahá'ís can choose between either a short prayer, which is said between noon and sunset; a medium obligatory prayer, which is recited in the morning, at noon, and in the evening; or a long prayer, which is recited once in twenty-four hours. Bahá'ís perform ablutions (the washing of the hands and face) before their prayers, and each prayer has specific instructions that go with it.

Bahá'ís also recite the phrase "Alláh-u-Abhá" (God the All-Glorious) ninety-five times each day.

Do Bahá'ís have confession?

Confession of sins and transgressions before human beings is not permissible, as it hath never been nor will ever be conducive to divine forgiveness. Moreover such confession before people results in one's humiliation and abasement, and God—exalted be His glory—wisheth not the humiliation of His servants.

*—Bahá'u'lláh**

Instead, Bahá'ís are required to bring themselves to account each day as part of their spiritual practice.

Every day, in the morning when arising you should compare today with yesterday and see in what condition you are. If you see your belief is stronger and your heart more occupied with God and your love increased and your freedom from the world greater, then thank God and ask for the increase of these qualities. You must begin to pray and repent for all that you have done which is wrong and you must implore and ask for help and assistance that you may become better than yesterday so that you may continue to make progress.

*— Attributed to 'Abdu'l-Bahá***

Do Bahá'ís fast?

Fasting is the act of not eating food, and sometimes also not drinking water, for a period of time in order to focus more on the non-physical side of life. Many, if not all, spiritual traditions of the past engage in some form of fasting. For example, Christians observe Lent, Muslims have Ramadan, and in Judaism there is Yom Kippur. Outside of the Abrahamic faiths, we see fasting in Lakota traditions and First Nations tribes in Canada, as well, and among many other Indigenous cultures worldwide.

The Bahá'í Fast lasts for nineteen days a year (one Bahá'í month) during which time Bahá'ís abstain from food and drink from sunrise to sunset.

> *[T]his physical fast is a symbol of the spiritual fast. This Fast leadeth to the cleansing of the soul from all selfish desires, the acquisition of spiritual attributes, attraction to the breezes of the All-Merciful, and enkindlement with the fire of divine love.*

—'Abdu'l-Bahá•

There are a number of exemptions to fasting, including anybody who is sick, breastfeeding, pregnant, menstruating, under the age of fifteen, or over the age of seventy.

Science is only just recently finding that fasting can have positive physical and mental effects. And yet while there are many physical benefits to fasting, the purpose of the Bahá'í Fast is to focus deeply on one's internal, spiritual life.

Is there any structure to the Bahá'í community?

The Bahá'í community organizes itself using a form of group leadership that was ordained by Bahá'u'lláh and is called the Administrative Order. This begins at the local level where Bahá'ís come together annually to elect people from their local community to form a nine-member Local Spiritual Assembly, which consults on matters concerning the community and its needs.

Local communities also elect delegates who then elect the nine-member National Spiritual Assembly, which oversees the functioning and well-being of the community on a national level.

At the international level, the members of the National Spiritual Assemblies from all over the world gather to elect the nine-member Universal House of Justice—the international governing body of the Bahá'ís of the world.

All elections are done by private ballot in a prayerful atmosphere, and no one is permitted to campaign or nominate individuals for election.

> *[T]he Spirit breathed by Bahá'u'lláh upon the world . . . can never permeate and exercise an abiding influence upon mankind unless and until it incarnates itself in a visible Order . . .*
>
> —*Shoghi Effendi*•

Do individual assembly members have power in the Bahá'í Faith?

Bahá'í institutions such as Local and National Spiritual Assemblies are available to Bahá'ís to help consult on difficult decisions and advise on the application of the Bahá'í writings to an individual's life where questions may come up. But the members of these assemblies can only do so as a group, and no individual has any "power" over another.

This democratic system of election creates a group of vastly decentralized servants to the Bahá'í community that help foster a vision for the community that is both intensely local in planning as well as global in scope.

At the highest level, the Universal House of Justice is responsible for guiding the activities for the global Bahá'í community, and while it can enact laws and ordinances not expressly recorded in the sacred writings, it cannot contradict, change, or omit any of the laws and writings of the Faith.

In short, every member serving on these institutions is just another Bahá'í engaged in service to the larger whole, and holds no power over another. Where in most systems of governance, we find ambition and competition, here we find service and cooperation, and collective, rather than individual, authority.

How do Bahá'ís make difficult decisions?

Settle all things, both great and small, by consultation. Without prior consultation, take no important step in your own personal affairs. Concern yourselves with one another. Help along one another's projects and plans.

—*'Abdu'l-Bahá**

In the Bahá'í Faith, there is a unique vision for decision-making called consultation. As there is no clergy, people are encouraged to consult with one another within their community. There are special guidelines though. 'Abdu'l-Bahá tells us that "the members who are consulting . . . should behave in the utmost love, harmony and sincerity towards each other." We are taught that once an idea is offered, it belongs to the group and is no longer the possession of the individual.

Another powerful guideline is:

It is better that all should agree on a wrong decision, than for one right vote to be singled out, inasmuch as single votes can be sources of dissension, which lead to ruin. Whereas, if in one case they take a wrong decision, in a hundred other cases they will adopt right decisions, and concord and unity are preserved. This will . . . eventually lead to the righting of the wrong.

—*'Abdu'l-Bahá***

Do Bahá'ís go to a church or temple every week?

For Bahá'ís, service and worship are integrated into everyday action, so there is not a single day designated for worship. But a similar community gathering called a "Feast" occurs on the first day of every nineteen-day Bahá'í month.

A Nineteen Day Feast is structured in three parts:

Devotions: The gathered community members read Bahá'í writings and prayers to attune themselves and open their hearts and calm their minds.

Administrative reporting and consultation: Everybody present consults on the concerns of the local community, and any matters raised are conveyed to the Local Spiritual Assembly.

Social portion: Food and drink is offered, and the participants hang out and enjoy each other's fellowship.

Bahá'ís can gather anywhere they choose. Nineteen Day Feasts can happen in a Bahá'í center, a House of Worship, a rented facility, or, more often than not, an individual's house, with a group of community members pitching in to prepare food and prepare the space for the gathering.

What is a House of Worship?

A Bahá'í House of Worship is a structure dedicated to worship and open to followers of any religion (or none)—a place for quiet contemplation, prayer, and meditation. The architecture for a House of Worship can be sometimes ornate and classical and sometimes very simple and modern, but they all are nine-sided structures, with nine pathways through nine gardens. Houses of Worship are buildings designed for the upliftment of the spirit and are offered to the wider community as a gift from the Bahá'ís.

Bahá'u'lláh envisioned a world wherein communities are structured around a House of Worship at the center—along with a complex including a hospital, a school, and other buildings for humanitarian and scientific pursuits.

Worldwide, as of 2025, fourteen Bahá'í Houses of Worship, including eight Mother Temples (one for each continent, Central America, and the Pacific Islands) and a handful of national and local Houses of Worship, have been built.

Do Bahá'ís have special holy days/holidays?

Yes, in fact Bahá'ís have a calendar called the Badí' Calendar (Badí' means *astonishing* or *wonderful*). The calendar consists of nineteen months of nineteen days. This only adds up to 361 days though, so at the end of every year there are four or five extra days. These days are used as a celebratory and gift-giving time between the second-to-last and last month of the year. During this last month of the year, which falls at the beginning of March in the Gregorian calendar, Bahá'ís take part in a fast (see page 79). The New Year then falls on the first day of Spring in the Northern Hemisphere.

Throughout the year, there are nine Holy Days. On these days Bahá'ís are excused from work and school, and celebrate or commemorate the historical significance of events such as the passing of Bahá'u'lláh or the birth of the Báb.

Each month of the year has a name, which in English are: Splendor, Glory, Beauty, Grandeur, Light, Mercy, Words, Perfection, Names, Might, Will, Knowledge, Power, Speech, Questions, Honor, Sovereignty, Dominion, and Loftiness.

How does the Bahá'í community pay for all its activities?

All Bahá'í properties and initiatives are funded by the Bahá'ís, who have the responsibility to give to the Bahá'í Fund. The unique thing about the Bahá'í Fund is that it is both an obligation and completely private. Like many things in the Bahá'í Faith (see obligatory prayer on pages 76–77) no one checks to confirm your participation even though it's an obligation. It's your business! Another unique aspect is that only Bahá'ís can contribute to the Fund. This means Bahá'ís are never asking others to donate to their cause.

Money from the Fund is used for the education of children, building Houses of Worship, teaching the Faith, putting on Holy Day celebrations—whatever a community decides it needs.

It is up to each individual to maintain their personal relationship with the laws. We are all unique, and our financial situations differ. There is no value given to how much a Bahá'í gives, only that they participate. This universal participation is another expression of oneness and unity.

> *[S]ince the donors offer them for the sake of God . . . if the offering be but a single grain it is regarded as the crowning glory of all the harvests of the world.*
>
> *—Bahá'u'lláh*•

Do Bahá'ís accept science?

Yes! One of the central teachings of the Bahá'í Faith is the harmony of science and religion. Ours is a spiritual life in a material realm. Given our dual existence as both material and spiritual beings, Bahá'ís are taught that the spiritual teachings of the Faith are the means to understand our spiritual reality, while the tools of science are our means to understand our material reality. These are complementary systems of knowledge, and neither should rule the other!

Religion and science are intertwined with each other and cannot be separated. These are the two wings with which humanity must fly. One wing is not enough. Every religion which does not concern itself with science is mere superstition.

Unquestionably there must be agreement between true religion and science. If a question be found contrary to reason, faith and belief in it are impossible.

—*'Abdu'l-Bahá*

Bahá'ís believe science is necessary to understand the world around us.

What about doctors?

In case of illness, He [Bahá'u'lláh] emphatically tells us, we should refer to the most competent physicians.

—*From a letter written on behalf of Shoghi Effendi**

As medical science advances, we continually learn more about the body and the ways in which diet can impact our health. This is emphasized in the Bahá'í writings.

It is, therefore, evident that it is possible to cure by foods, aliments and fruits; but as today the science of medicine is imperfect, this fact is not yet fully grasped. When the science of medicine reaches perfection, treatment will be given by foods, aliments, fragrant fruits and vegetables.

—*'Abdu'l-Bahá***

We are instructed in the Bahá'í Faith to understand the importance of our physical health in relation to our capacity to be of service, for if we are not in our own peak physical condition, we cannot give our unique contribution to humanity as a whole.

Do Bahá'ís care about the environment?

Yes! We are all interdependent with the environment and we must care for it.

The natural world, in all its wonder and majesty, offers profound insight into the essence of interdependence. From the biosphere as a whole to the smallest micro-organism, it demonstrates how dependent any one life-form is on numerous others—and how imbalances in one system reverberate across an interconnected whole.

—*Bahá'í International Community**

Part of our interdependence with the environment is the food we eat!

Agriculture and the preservation of the ecological balance of the world are of fundamental interest. . . .

—*The Universal House of Justice***

In the Bahá'í writings we find a special appreciation for agriculture, and while the Faith is not specifically designed to be organized in a rural social structure, the importance of food to our prosperity is pretty clear: we all need food to survive.

And what about animals?

Bahá'í teachings tell us that animals do have a spirit, but it is not the same as that of humans.

> *[U]nlike the animal, man has a rational soul, the human intelligence. This intelligence of man is the intermediary between his body and his spirit.*

*—'Abdu'l-Bahá**

As we have discussed earlier, humanity is the only group of creatures that has the capacity to reflect ALL the attributes of God. While that is a gift, it also means we have a great responsibility to take care of not only the environment and plants of the earth, but also the animals.

> *[W]here the animal spirit is concerned, the self-same feelings are shared by animal and man . . . But the hapless beast is mute, able neither to express its hurt nor take its case to the authorities. . . . Therefore it is essential that ye show forth the utmost consideration to the animal, and that ye be even kinder to him than to your fellow man. Train your children from their earliest days to be infinitely tender and loving to animals.*

*—'Abdu'l-Bahá***

How can I become a Bahá'í?

Simply put, a Bahá'í is someone who believes that Bahá'u'lláh is the Messenger of God for this day and strives to put His teachings into action in their lives. Anyone can do that, and many people do.

The Bahá'ís must be distinguished from others of humanity. But this distinction must not depend upon wealth . . . you must become distinguished in all the virtues of the human world—for faithfulness and sincerity, for justice and fidelity, . . . for philanthropic deeds and service to the human world, for love toward every human being, for removing prejudices and promoting international peace. Finally, you must become distinguished for heavenly illumination and for acquiring the bestowals of God.

—'Abdu'l-Bahá•

In order to be a registered Bahá'í, you have to officially sign up to be a member of the Bahá'í community in your local area.

However, you don't need to be a registered Bahá'í to get involved at the community level. If you are interested in exploring the community-building activities covered in this book, you can simply reach out to the Bahá'ís in your area and join in!

Go deeper and learn more at Bahai.org or Bahai.us
https://www.bahai.us/contact/become-a-bahai/

Sources

INTRODUCTORY QUOTATION

- 'Abdu'l-Bahá, *Paris Talks*, no. 1.7.

LET'S TALK ABOUT THE BASICS

What is the Bahá'í Faith?

- Bahá'u'lláh, *Tablets of Bahá'u'lláh*, no. 11.12

What does unity mean?

- Bahá'u'lláh, *The Summons of the Lord of Hosts*, no. 5.4.

Is the Bahá'í Faith a sect of another religion?

- 'Abdu'l-Bahá, *The Promulgation of Universal Peace*, no. 56.3.

Who or What is God?

- 'Abdu'l-Bahá, *Paris Talks*, no. 5.10.

Can we know God?

- 'Abdu'l-Bahá, *'Abdu'l-Bahá in London*, no. 13.17.

What is our place in relation to God?

- 'Abdu'l-Bahá, *Selections from the Writings of 'Abdu'l-Bahá*, no. 21.3.

Do Bahá'ís have priests?

- 'Abdu'l-Bahá, *The Promulgation of Universal Peace*, no. 128.7.

Are there Bahá'í monks?

* Bahá'u'lláh, *Epistle to the Son of the Wolf*, ¶83.

** Bahá'u'lláh, *Tablets of Bahá'u'lláh*, no. 3.20.

What is prayer?

- The Universal House of Justice, from a letter dated 18 December 2014 to the Bahá'ís in Iran.

·· 'Abdu'l-Bahá, *Paris Talks*, no. 54.12.

How do Bahá'ís pray?

- Bahá'u'lláh, *The Kitáb-i-Aqdas*, ¶149.

What's so special about religious texts?

- Bahá'u'lláh, *Gleanings from the Writings of Bahá'u'lláh*, no. 74.1.

·· Bahá'u'lláh, *Tablets of Bahá'u'lláh*, no. 9.10

SOCIETY

Is the world falling apart?

- Shoghi Effendi, *Unfolding Destiny*, no. 2.95.8.

Is world peace possible? Can we save humanity?

- Shoghi Effendi, *The World Order of Bahá'u'lláh*, no. 3.33.

·· Bahá'u'lláh, *Tablets of Bahá'u'lláh*, no. 7.20.

What is the oneness of humanity?

- 'Abdu'l-Bahá, *The Promulgation of Universal Peace*, no. 98.6.

·· Bahá'í International Community, *The Prosperity of Humankind*, ¶14.

If all religions are one, then why do they seem so different?

- T'ai Shang Kan Ying P'ien; Exodus 20:13; Qur'an 2:188.

·· The Báb, *Selections from the Writings of the Báb*, no. 3.34.

If all the religions are one, then how many gods are there?

- ·	'Abdu'l-Bahá, *Paris Talks*, no. 15.1–2.

Why do people of different religions not get along?

- ·	'Abdu'l-Bahá, *The Promulgation of Universal Peace*, no. 80.5.
- ··	'Abdu'l-Bahá, *The Promulgation of Universal Peace*, no. 56.3.

Why do we need a new religion?

- ·	Shoghi Effendi, *The World Order of Bahá'u'lláh*, no. 7.106.

Are there Bahá'í politicians?

- ·	Shoghi Effendi, *Directives from the Guardian*, no. 153.2.

What about war?

- ·	'Abdu'l-Bahá, *The Promulgation of Universal Peace*, no. 47.1.
- ··	'Abdu'l-Bahá, *Selections from the Writings of 'Abdu'l-Bahá*, no. 227.13.
- ···	'Abdu'l-Bahá, *The Promulgation of Universal Peace*, no. 96.12.

What is justice?

- ·	Bahá'u'lláh, *Tablets of Bahá'u'lláh*, no. 6.25.
- ··	'Abdu'l-Bahá, *Some Answered Questions*, no. 77.3.

Is equality possible when everybody is so different?

- ·	'Abdu'l-Bahá, *Paris Talks*, no. 15.7.
- ··	'Abdu'l-Bahá, *The Promulgation of Universal Peace*, no. 134.2.

What is prejudice?

- ·	'Abdu'l-Bahá, *The Promulgation of Universal Peace*, no. 16.1.
- ··	The Universal House of Justice, message dated Ridván 2008, to the Bahá'ís of the World.

What does the Bahá'í Faith say about racism?

- * Shoghi Effendi, *The Advent of Divine Justice*, ¶51.
- ** 'Abdu'l-Bahá, quoted in Shoghi Effendi, *Citadel of Faith*, no. 126.
- *** From a letter of Zia Bagdadi to Alfred Lunt, 10 June 1921, in *Star of the West*, vol. 7, p. 120.
- **** Shoghi Effendi, *The Advent of Divine Justice*, ¶58.
- ***** The Universal House of Justice, Message to the Peoples of the World, October 1985.

Do Bahá'ís care about the equality of the sexes?

- * 'Abdu'l-Bahá, *The Promulgation of Universal Peace*, no. 32.7.
- ** 'Abdu'l-Bahá, *Paris Talks*, no. 40.33.
- *** 'Abdu'l-Bahá, quoted in J. E. Esslemont, *Bahá'u'lláh and the New Era*, p. 149.
- **** 'Abdu'l-Bahá, *The Promulgation of Universal Peace*, no. 113.13.
- ***** 'Abdu'l-Bahá, *The Promulgation of Universal Peace*, no. 46.11.

COMMUNITY

What is Bahá'í life/culture like?

- * 'Abdu'l-Bahá, *The Secret of Divine Civilization*, ¶5.

Why have a religious community?

- * Office of Public Affairs, US Bahá'í National Organization, https://www.bahai.us/public-affairs/focus-areas/race/.

What are children's classes?

- ʻAbdu'l-Bahá, *Selections from the Writings of ʻAbdu'l-Bahá*, no. 106.1.
- ʻAbdu'l-Bahá, in *Lights of Guidance*, no. 8.503.1.

What are junior youth groups?

- The Universal House of Justice, Message to the Bahá'ís of the World, Ridván 2010.

What about older teenagers and young adults?

- The Universal House of Justice, message, dated 1 July 2013, to participants at 114 youth conferences taking place throughout the world.

What about devotional gatherings?

- ʻAbdu'l-Bahá, quoted in J. E. Esslemont, *Bahá'u'lláh and the New Era*, p. 93.

What is service?

- ʻAbdu'l-Bahá, *The Promulgation of Universal Peace*, no. 3.2.
- Bahá'u'lláh, *Tablets of Bahá'u'lláh*, no. 3.20.

What about us as individuals?

- From a letter written on behalf of Shoghi Effendi, dated 17 February 1933, in *Compilation of Compilations*, vol. 1, pp. 84–85.

INDIVIDUAL

Who am I?

- ʻAbdu'l-Bahá, *Paris Talks*, no. 2.2.

What is the soul?

*   'Abdu'l-Bahá, *Paris Talks*, no. 29.13.

What is the purpose of life?

*   'Abdu'l-Bahá, *The Promulgation of Universal Peace*, no. 81.3.
** Bahá'u'lláh, *Tablets of Bahá'u'lláh*, no. 9.4.

How do we develop our attributes and virtues?

*   'Abdu'l-Bahá, quoted in Shoghi Effendi, *The Advent of Divine Justice*, ¶40.

What's the deal with the body?

*   'Abdu'l-Bahá, quoted in J. E. Esslemont, *Bahá'u'lláh and the New Era*, p. 106.
** From a letter written on behalf of Shoghi Effendi to an individual, dated 12 March 1934, in *Lights of Guidance*, no. 24.927.1.

What is the ego?

*   'Abdu'l-Bahá, in *Star of the West*, vol. 6, p. 126.
** Bahá'u'lláh, *The Kitáb-i-íqán*, ¶8.

What are mental health and mental illness?

*   From a letter written on behalf of Shoghi Effendi to an individual, dated 12 April 1948, in *Lights of Guidance*, no. 24.948.1.

Is there life after death?

*   Bahá'u'lláh, *Gleanings from the Writings of Bahá'u'lláh*, no. 81.2.
** From a letter written on behalf of Shoghi Effendi to an individual, dated 22 April 1944, in *Lights of Guidance*, no. 1055.1.

Why do bad things happen?

- Bahá'u'lláh, *Gleanings from the Writings of Bahá'u'lláh*, no. 130.1.
- 'Abdu'l-Bahá, in *Star of the West*, vol. 14, no. 2, p. 41.

Does evil exist?

- 'Abdu'l-Bahá, *Some Answered Questions*, no. 74.6.

What is our intelligence for?

- 'Abdu'l-Bahá, *The Promulgation of Universal Peace*, no. 26.7.
- 'Abdu'l-Bahá, *Paris Talks*, no. 2.1.
- 'Abdu'l-Bahá, *Paris Talks*, no. 6.7.
- Shoghi Effendi, *Directives from the Guardian*, no. 47.2.

What about sexuality?

- Shoghi Effendi, from a letter to an individual, dated 21 November 1947, in *Light of Guidance*, no. 77.1.

What does the Bahá'í Faith say about gender identity?

- From a letter written on behalf of the Universal House of Justice to a National Spiritual Assembly, dated 30 March 2017.

Can we judge others?

- 'Abdu'l-Bahá, quoted in a letter written on behalf of the Universal House of Justice, dated 13 August 1980, in *Lights of Guidance*, no. 2.309.1.
- Bahá'u'lláh, *The Kitáb-i-íqán*, ¶214.

Can we compare ourselves to others?

- Bahá'u'lláh, *The Kitáb-i-íqán*, ¶213.

So, we're just supposed to be nice and offer help to everyone?

- 'Abdu'l-Bahá, *The Promulgation of Universal Peace*, no. 134.2.

MORE TEACHINGS

Does the Bahá'í Faith have any rules?

- Bahá'u'lláh, in *The Importance of Obligatory Prayer and Fasting*, no. 14.
- •• The Universal House of Justice, from a letter to the Bahá'ís of the United States, dated 29 December 1988.

Do Bahá'ís have to pray?

- From a letter written on behalf of Shoghi Effendi to an individual, dated 19 October 1925, in *Prayer and Devotional Life*, no. 29.
- •• Bahá'u'lláh, *The Kitáb-i-Aqdas*, ¶149.

Do Bahá'ís have confession?

- Bahá'u'lláh, *Tablets of Bahá'u'lláh*, no. 3.12.
- •• 'Abdu'l-Bahá, in *Star of the West*, vol. 8, no. 6, p. 68.

Do Bahá'ís fast?

- 'Abdu'l-Bahá, in *The Importance of Obligatory Prayer and Fasting*, no. 26.

Is there any structure to the Bahá'í community? (Who makes decisions in the community?)

- Shoghi Effendi, *The World Order of Bahá'u'lláh*, no. 2.10.

How do Bahá'ís make difficult decisions?

- 'Abdu'l-Bahá, From a Tablet translated from the Persian, in *Consultation.*
- •• 'Abdu'l-Bahá, From a Tablet translated from the Persian, in *Consultation.*

How does the Bahá'í community pay for all its activities?

- Bahá'u'lláh, in *Ḥuqúqu'lláh—The Right of God*, no. 7.

Do Bahá'ís accept science?

- 'Abdu'l-Bahá, *'Abdu'l-Bahá in London*, no. 3.13.

What about doctors?

- From a letter written on behalf of Shoghi Effendi to an individual, dated 17 July 1937, in *Lights of Guidance*, no. 24.991.1.
- •• 'Abdu'l-Bahá, *Some Answered Questions*, no. 73.7.

Do Bahá'ís care about the environment?

- Bahá'í International Community, *One Planet, One Habitation*, p. 1.
- •• The Universal House of Justice, from a letter to the Association for Bahá'í Studies, dated 31 March 1985.

And what about animals?

- 'Abdu'l-Bahá, *Paris Talks*, no. 31.3–4.
- •• 'Abdu'l-Bahá, *Selections from the Writings of 'Abdu'l-Bahá*, no. 138.2.

How can I become a Bahá'í?

- 'Abdu'l-Bahá, *The Promulgation of Universal Peace*, no. 68.4.

Bibliography

Works of Bahá'u'lláh

Epistle to the Son of the Wolf. New ed. Translated by Shoghi Effendi. 1st ps ed. Wilmette, IL: Bahá'í Publishing Trust, 1988.

Gleanings from the Writings of Bahá'u'lláh. 1st ps ed. Translated by Shoghi Effendi. Wilmette, IL: Bahá'í Publishing, 2005.

The Kitáb-i-Aqdas: The Most Holy Book. 1st ps ed. Wilmette, IL: Bahá'í Publishing Trust, 1993.

The Kitáb-i-Íqán: The Book of Certitude. 1st pocket-size ed. Translated by Shoghi Effendi. Wilmette, IL.: Bahá'í Publishing Trust, 2003.

The Summons of the Lord of Hosts, Tablets of Bahá'u'lláh. Wilmette, IL: Bahá'í Publishing, 2006.

Tablets of Bahá'u'lláh revealed after the Kitáb-i-Aqdas. 1st pocket-size ed. Compiled by the Research Department of the Universal House of Justice. Translated by Habib Taherzadeh et al. Wilmette, IL: Bahá'í Publishing Trust, 1988.

Works of the Báb

Selections from the Writings of the Báb. Compiled by the Research Department of the Universal House of Justice. Translated by Habib Taherzadeh et al. Wilmette, IL: Bahá'í Publishing Trust, 2006.

Works of 'Abdu'l-Bahá

'Abdu'l-Bahá in London: Addresses & Notes of Conversations. London: Bahá'í Publishing Trust, 1987.

Paris Talks: Addresses Given by 'Abdu'l-Bahá in Paris in 1911. Wilmette, IL: Bahá'í Publishing, 2011.

The Promulgation of Universal Peace: Talks Delivered by 'Abdu'l-Bahá during His Visit to the United States and Canada in 1912. Compiled by Howard MacNutt. 2nd ed. Wilmette, IL: Bahá'í Publishing, 2012.

The Secret of Divine Civilization. Translated by Marzieh Gail and Ali-Kuli Khan. Wilmette, IL: Bahá'í Publishing, 2007.

Selections from the Writings of 'Abdu'l-Bahá. Compiled by the Research Department of the Universal House of Justice. Translated by a Committee at the Bahá'í World Center and Marzieh Gail. Wilmette, IL: Bahá'í Publishing, 2010.

Some Answered Questions. Newly translated by a Committee at the Bahá'í World Center. Haifa, Israel: Bahá'í World Centre, 2014.

Works of Shoghi Effendi

The Advent of Divine Justice. 1st pocket-size ed. Wilmette, IL: Bahá'í Publishing Trust, 1990.

Citadel of Faith: Messages to America, 1947–1957. Wilmette, IL: Bahá'í Publishing Trust, 1965.

Directives from the Guardian. New Delhi: Bahá'í Publishing Trust, 1973.

The Unfolding Destiny of the British Bahá'í Community: The Messages from the Guardian of the Bahá'í Faith to the Bahá'ís of the British Isles. London: Bahá'í Publishing Trust, 1981.

The World Order of Bahá'u'lláh: Selected Letters. New ed. Wilmette, IL.: Bahá'í Publishing Trust, 1991.

Bahá'í Compilations

The Compilation of Compilations: Prepared by the Universal House of Justice, 1963–1990. 2 vols. Australia: Bahá'í Publications Australia, 1991.

Consultation: A Compilation. Prepared by the Research Department of the Universal House of Justice. Haifa: Bahá'í World Centre, 1990.

Ḥuqúqu'lláh—The Right of God. A Compilation of Extracts from the Writings of Bahá'u'lláh and 'Abdu'l-Bahá and from Letters Written by and on Behalf of Shoghi Effendi and the Universal House of Justice. Haifa: Bahá'í World Centre, 2009.

Lights of Guidance: A Bahá'í Reference File. Compiled by Helen Hornby. New ed. New Delhi, India: Bahá'í Publishing Trust, 1994.

Prayer and Devotional Life: A Compilation of Extracts from the Writings of Bahá'u'lláh, the Báb, and 'Abdu'lBahá and the Letters of Shoghi Effendi and the Universal House of Justice. Prepared by the Research Department of the Universal House of Justice, February 2019. Wilmette, IL: Bahá'í Publishing, 2019.

Other Works

Bahá'í International Community. *One Planet, One Habitation: A Bahá'í Perspective on Recasting Humanity's Relationship with the Natural World.* A statement of the Bahá'í International Community, 1 June 2022.

Bahá'í International Community. "The Prosperity of Humankind." A statement prepared by the Bahá'í International Community Office of Public Information, Haifa, first distributed at the United Nations World Summit on Social Development, Copenhagen, Denmark, 3 March 1995.

Esslemont, J. E. *Bahá'u'lláh and the New Era: An Introduction to the Bahá'í Faith.* 5th rev. ed. Wilmette, IL: Bahá'í Publishing, 2010.

Star of the West, multiple volumes.